ELMA FRANCOIS
THE NWCSA AND
THE WORKERS' STRUGGLE FOR CHANGE
IN THE CARIBBEAN IN THE 1930s

ELMA FRANCOIS

the NWCSA

and the worker's struggle

for change in the Caribbean

by

Rhoda Reddock

New Beacon Books
London ■ Port of Spain

First published 1988
by New Beacon Books Ltd.,
76 Stroud Green Road, London N4 3EN, England.

© 1988 Rhoda Reddock

ISBN: 0 901241 79 2 (hardback)
       0 901241 80 6 (paperback)

Printed by Villiers Publications Ltd., 26a Shepherds Hill,
London N6 5AH.

To Jim, Christina, Dudley
and Con

CONTENTS

Introduction

This short biography of Elma Francois 1897-1944, reveals to us a remarkable woman. It is possible that the colonial history, written in the past, would have regarded Elma Francois as another passing rabble rouser. In the recovery of our people's history however, this unheralded woman stands out as a fighter of heroic proportions, consumed by the need to do her duty simply, lovingly and without let up. Many who have had to migrate from their islands under the pressure of nature and society will be grateful for Rhoda Reddock's portrait of a comrade and a sister who made history within the different circumstances that were given to her, as they are given to others.

The surname 'Francois', and the place where her family came from — Overland, cf. 'oversea' — these two factors suggest that Elma Francois had 'Carib blood'. This section of the Vincentian community had been violated in colonial wars and put at the bottom of the social ladder. A hurricane in 1898 and a volcanic eruption in 1902 severely ravaged the area and laid waste the land, livestock, sugar factory and other means of production. Thrown then to the bottom of the economic ladder, the Francois family broke up and moved to less hostile areas of St. Vincent. Sion Hill on the brow of Kingstown, the capital, was Elma's first promised land. It was a settlement of workers for the surrounding estates as well as for the shops, homes, port and other workplaces of Kingstown. The hard experiences of workers on the estates and in the town would be common knowledge in Sion Hill. The then settlement was also well placed to pick up and interpret any stirring of ideas in the capital. It is interesting to speculate that the visit of Marcus Garvey to St. Vincent may have made some impression on the young Elma Francois. Outside of Kingstown, a Garveyite group was formed in the village of Stubbs, where other members of the Francois family had settled.

Those of us who are part of a continuing struggle for eman-

1

cipation cannot afford the fantasy of thinking that the strong sense of purpose of Elma Francois fell into her head from the sky. It was Elma's experiences and initiatives as a social being which brought about the development of her ideas. If Elma Francois' primary school education and her re-education by experience moulded her into such a stalwart figure, then you, I and Caribbean working people have a profound progressive reservoir to draw on which has not yet been tapped.

What impresses me most from this account of the life and struggles of Elma Francois is the powerful sense of discipline, single-mindedness and caring that is evident in all the modes and aspects of her living. Whether as parent, peer leader, or political partner, Elma is gripped by a consistent sense of responsibility, a sense of class and an acute sense of the political which is not sectarian or exclusive. Her social experience/relations as a woman must have been an important element in the final formation of her truly revolutionary discipline.

The decision of Elma Francois' son to enlist in the British army was a fatal blow to her. The painful effect which it had on her testifies both to the strength of her political convictions and the power of the family bond for her. Evidently she saw her son's decision as a very personal failure on her part. It struck at the very core of her sense of duty.

The glimpses into Elma's educational and organising tactics and work give me quite a thrill, close as some of it is to the experiences shared by many of us today. Courage, vigour and enthusiasm are implied in Elma's animating a discussion among limers and people on the block. The same is true as she transforms information gathered from reading into intellectual resource for use by NWCSA in study or decision making. Again her inspiration of others, by example and moral force so that they also become powered by the cause, reveals a dynamic leader with an infectious warmth which set her comrades and colleagues aglow.

In her role as a political partner and ally, we can see that Elma Francois showed a personal concern for the development and the security of those in whose company she struggled. Her comrades 'looked up' to her for leadership. The organisation required that men and women co-operate in developing their collective political consciousness — instituting a dynamic relationship between the sexes. One cannot but help suggest again that the manysided relations in the social organisation of labour which are the lot of Caribbean women — strong arm defender of the rest, reproducer of labour power, comforter, culturiser, and producer — strengthened Elma Francois and the other women activists in the NWCSA. Elma did not hold back from working with others even though there were some differences between them. She could see the larger oppression on which they were agreed and did not make the smaller conflict become an obstacle in the fight for the people to advance.

This study by Rhoda Reddock of the life and struggle of sister Elma Francois and the NWCSA uncovers another page in the long book of struggle for emancipation which our working people have been waging. The focus on Elma Francois is welcome. It reassures us of the strength, intelligence and human resources of the oppressed and the doubly oppressed. We know that the future, resting in the hands of committed and conscious working people, is indeed a secure future. The historical profile of the NWCSA permits us to view with pride our revolutionary parents fighting concrete battles in the war of race, class, gender and colony. Armed with this portrait of Elma Francois, we can compare her features with those of her contemporaries and measure our own and our contemporaries' convictions and heroism with more humility.

'History,' says one writer, 'does not declare itself, its message must be uncovered.' I am grateful to Sister Rhoda Reddock for the messages uncovered and yet to be uncovered by the viewers of this portrait.

Earlene Horne
Kingstown
St. Vincent
April 8, 1987

CHAPTER 1

Why Elma Francois?

This study is the first in a series of political histories of women in Trinidad and Tobago. It is the result of research and investigation into the lost history of women and of the popular classes and movements of this century. The middle-strata nationalist movements of the 1950s, culminating in the concretization of the two racially defined electoral political parties — the Peoples National Movement and the Democratic Labour Party — for at least twenty-five years sought to nullify the political developments and contributions of popular movements prior to their emergence.

Together with the suppression of the radical and labour-oriented tradition of political struggle of the pre-1950 period, there has also been the obliteration of the memory of the hundreds of women who contributed to the struggles and movements, the benefits of which we enjoy today.

Of these women Elma Francois and the movement through which she dedicated her life to the people — the Negro Welfare Cultural and Social Association (NWCSA) — are prime examples. Francois, and many others, contributed in her short life (1897-1944) to the improvement of our lives in ways which this publication will only begin to explore.

Elma Francois as well as her other colleagues give the lie to myths about the acceptance of colonial and racial domination among the working classes and to the lack of political consciousness and action among women. They illustrate clearly the ways in which people, who could hardly afford to, were willing to and in fact dared to defy the racist colonial authorities in defence of the rights of poor people.

It is only recently that recognition has been afforded the NWCSA in the political history of this country, most clearly in the work of Bukka Rennie. Trinidad and Tobago labour history has been dominated by the figures of T.U.B. Butler and A.A. Cipriani. It is hoped that this study can help to

4

place the important, but far less recognised, contribution of the NWCSA and its leading women and men members to the labour and political history of Trinidad and Tobago.

The NWCSA, of which Elma Francois was a founding member, was responsible for the formation of three major trade unions, two of which have survived to the present — the Seamen and Waterfront Workers' Trade Union (SWWTU) and the Federated Workers' Trade Union (FWTU) now part of the National Union of Government and Federated Workers (NUGFW). The NWCSA was largely responsible for fomenting the national response against the Italian invasion of Ethiopia in 1935 led by Mussolini. In the early 1930s, during the post-war economic depression, their 'Hunger Marches' of the unemployed established a pattern of organisation and agitation later used by T.U.B. Butler in his abortive 'Hunger March' to Port of Spain in 1935 and by sugar workers in Central Trinidad, who in July 1934 staged a series of 'Hunger Marches' to protest their deteriorating conditions on the sugar estates.

The NWCSA was also responsible for conscientizing many middle-strata young men to their African roots as well as to the necessity for political struggle against colonial domination. More details on these and other information on the NWCSA will be given later in this study. It is necessary however at the onset to clarify the position of this organisation on race relations in Trinidad and Tobago, bearing in mind its name which gives it a clearly racial definition.

In his pamphlet *The Politics of Communalism*,[1] John Gaffar La Guerre noted that in spite of the NWCSA's anti-fascist, socialist, anti-imperialist and pro-working-class position it:

> ... suffered from one severe limitation. While its motto urged 'Workers of the World Unite' the Association was preoccupied almost exclusively with the 'Negro race'.

The author went on to selectively quote four out of the eleven 'Aims of the Negro Welfare Cultural and Social Association' pertaining to the oppression of 'Negro People' (see Appendix I), ignoring the other seven which dealt with the collective responses of all working people to their colonial and local oppressors. As will be seen in this pamphlet, unlike

5

other racially defined organisations then, and in our own time today, the definition of this organisation in racial terms was not done in opposition to the predominantly poor, peasant, working-class or unemployed Indians of that period. The adoption of the term 'Negro' as a definitive term in the 1930s was an affirmation of racial pride among New World African ex-slaves and a rejection of the self-hate and *denigration* (the real meaning of this term) of people of African descent in the New World. This affirmation and self-acceptance among New World ex-slaves was a necessary pre-condition for cooperating in solidarity with other oppressed groups within the society. There have been narrow cultural organisations of Africans in Trinidad and Tobago but the NWCSA was not one of these. In fact this study would go further to suggest that in rural areas, during the pre-1940s period, solidarity between the working classes of both major ethnic groups, African and Indian, were in some ways more cordial than at present. It is the increasing power of the middle-strata members of both races which, then as now, seeks to use the politics of race and religion in order to justify their control over the masses of people.

As an organisation based in urban Port of Spain, the NWCSA represented the interests of its majority constituents. As will be seen however, the daily struggles of the NWCSA were always linked to developments in the Caribbean regionally and internationally, especially in a reality where large numbers of the poor African and Indian working-class were first generation migrants from other countries in the Caribbean and further afield.

In the case of Elma Francois, another important factor to note is the important contribution of migrants from other Caribbean territories to radical and revolutionary politics of that time. Francois, like many prominent political activists in Trinidad early in this century, was born in another Caribbean territory. Like J. Sidney de Bourg (Grenada), Richard Braithwaite (Grenada) and Albertha Husbands (Barbados) of the early Trinidad Workingmen's Association (TWA) and T.U.B. Butler (Grenada), they all lived under constant threat of deportation, as was the case with de Bourg after the 1919 strike.

6

While the events of 1937 itself have usually been high-lighted by historians, the entire decade of the 1930s — beginning with the 1934 Sugar Workers Strike and Disturbances, 1935 Apex Strike, 1935 Abyssinian War agitation culminating in the 1937 General Strike and disturbances — was all part of a groundswell of working-class activity against colonialism and in the interests of their social advancement and survival.

These events, together with similar events in other parts of the region, resulted in major changes in the approach of the British colonial government to the administration of its colonies. More importantly it ushered in the development of trade unions as we know them today.

In the island of St. Vincent, the country of her birth, Elma Francois' activities are even less well known. Yet her struggles on behalf of working people began there. This study therefore is of significance not only to Trinidad and Tobago but also to St. Vincent and the Grenadines, and to Barbados. It is hoped however that these shared histories of our foremothers and other forerunners can serve to open up the possibilities of the potential of Caribbean women to change their own lives and that of their people, in this way transforming the existing exploitative relations among human beings in Caribbean society.

CHAPTER II

The St. Vincent Years

Elma Constance Francois was born on the 14th October 1897, in Overland on the windward side of St. Vincent. She was the daughter of Estina Francois (neé Silby) and Stanley Francois whose occupation was recorded as labourer. After an early life in the windward area, her parents lost most of their belongings during the volcanic eruption of 1902 and were relocated in the Sion Hill area in Kingstown.

Growing up in Kingstown, Francois joined her mother, especially after her father died, in picking cotton in the fields of the Arnos Vale and Cane Garden estates. In spite of her youthfulness, Francois displayed a remarkable concern for the suffering and way of life and work of her people. She had received primary education up to 5th standard and so could read and write with reasonable skill.

According to Jim Barrette, her long time friend, comrade and companion, Francois would sit and talk to him for hours about the conditions of life of poor people in rural St. Vincent. For women, very few options existed for earning a living. Some could work picking the dry cotton chaff and separating the seeds. For this they could earn up to 12 or 14 cents a day. Others worked as domestic servants, while for some work could be found producing syrup or 'sweetening' in the Mt. Bentick sugar factory. Those who were left eked out a living by cultivating and selling 'groundnuts' (peanuts) or migrated to the town, Kingstown, and possibly to Trinidad and Tobago, then perceived as the land of prosperity.

This awareness of the conditions of life stimulated Elma Francois into action. She attempted to organise the workers at the Mt. Bentick sugar factory and for this she was fired. In Kingstown she became acquainted with the Vincentian druggist and politician, George Augustus McIntosh. McIntosh was born in Kingstown in 1886, son of Donald McIntosh, a Scotsman, and Charlotte Glasgow, a cook. In February 1919,

8

McIntosh was a founding member of the St. Vincent Representative Government Association, the movement which
sought the introduction of elected representation in the local
legislature. McIntosh later went on to form the St. Vincent
Workingmen's Cooperative Association in 1936.

McIntosh, in spite of or because of his ancestry, was in-
tensely aware of the oppressive conditions under which the
majority of the black population lived. According to Barrette,
however, McIntosh was seen in the society as 'good but godless'. He challenged the scriptures *and* the power of the established church. In particular, he is remembered for his defence
of the 'Shakers', members of the Spiritual Baptist religion. In
this, Francois and McIntosh could make common cause as
she also questioned the dominance of religious forces in
general over the lives of poor people.

In 1917 Francois gave birth to her first son Conrad. His
father Albert James, also of Sion Hill, left St. Vincent just
prior to his son's birth to fight in World War I. After the war he
landed in Port of Spain, Trinidad, and settled there.

In 1919, at about 22 years of age, Francois herself migrated
to Trinidad and Tobago leaving her 18-month old son in the
care of his grandmother in St. Vincent.

CHAPTER III

The Early Years in Trinidad and Tobago

In Trinidad, Francois worked first as a domestic servant with
the Stollmeyers of upper Charlotte Street, Port of Spain, and
almost instinctively she became a member of the Trinidad
Workingmen's Association (TWA), then led by Captain Arthur
Andrew Cipriani. The TWA had been originally formed in 1897,
and was re-vitalised in 1906 by Alfred Richards whose leadership was challenged by a more radical grouping in 1913. In
1920 many of the leading members were deported after the
strikes and labour disturbances of 1919. In 1923, Cipriani, a
former member of the West Indian contingent to World War I,
was asked by the then TWA President W. Howard-Bishop to
assume its leadership. This he did and remained its leader until
his death in 1945. In 1934 the TWA was transformed into the
Trinidad Labour Party (TLP).

Unlike other women members of the TWA/TLP, Francois did
not limit herself to political activity as defined within the con-
straints of the TWA/TLP. Cipriani, like McIntosh, in spite of his
'whiteness' took a public position in support of the working
class. However he deplored direct action and believed that the
forces of capital and labour could be made to accommodate to
each other through his negotiation and moral suasion on behalf
of the oppressed poor or 'barefoot man' as he referred to them.

Francois' approach was quite different. For her political
activity meant working among the people. Her interest in politics and in reading, by candlelight late into the night, provided
her with the fuel needed for her 'rap sessions' and political
speeches at various spots in Port of Spain. One of the favourite
places was La Cour Harpe (Harpe Place). In the words of Jim
Barrette, 'we used to sit under the breadfruit tree and she would
talk to us all day'. In fact this was how they met. Barrette described how: 'I first saw her one night at a TLP meeting at the
corner of Quarry and Observatory Street. She spoke on the
platform with Julian Braithwaite. She had a good voice and was

10

an explicit speaker. I was fascinated by the way she put it. She was strong on things African ... one day she gave me a book on the French Revolution to read and asked me to bring other friends.' Jim admits to having had no previous political or public speaking interest over and above his involvement in recitation while at school. He was also quite content to leave it up to 'whites' like Cipriani. He went on, 'she looked at me and she talked to me'. I said to her 'where you learn all this?' She replied: 'You must read, and you mustn't read stupidness. Look around you, do you think that this is the right way for people to live? Look at those Indians sleeping on the ground ... Those Church people talking, but you think God meant people to live like this?'

Francois would also go to Woodford Square and 'take on any group of fellas'. Her approach was to sit on a bench next to perfect strangers and use the newspaper to start political discussions. In various areas of the town, on street corners, she would enquire about its history and the living conditions. In this way she met Jim Headley who later became a founding member of the NWCSA.

As a member of the TWA Francois was sometimes a speaker at political meetings. On one such occasion, at Liberty Hall on Prince Street, she challenged Cipriani on the question of May Day which she felt should be declared a public holiday in honour of workers.

In Trinidad and Tobago in the 1930s the TWA/TLP organised huge May Day celebrations with a march and rally in Port of Spain. Following the British Labour Party tradition, these celebrations usually took place on the Sunday closest to May 1st, so as not to disturb the normal working day.

Although leaving her son in St. Vincent, Francois sought every possibility to maintain contact with him. Every other week young 'Con' would stand on the hill overlooking the harbour to look for the 'sloop' or 'schooner' which would bring a parcel from her to him. Every letter received by his grandmother would have enclosed in it a postal money order, so much so that the post office personnel soon became well acquainted with 'Con'. In this way Francois sought to make up for the years of being away from her only son. Another son, born 3-4 years after Con, died while still an infant. In school Con was referred to as 'Trini', because of the complement of Trinidadian items — clothes, shoes and other things which he owned.

Around 1926-1927 Elma Francois returned to St. Vincent to visit her son. Con looked forward to seeing her almost for the first time in his life and recognised her instantly as she stepped off the boat. It was then about seven years since she had last seen her son.

It was on this occasion that mother and son first began to know each other and she promised to send for him although his grandmother 'tantie' was not very much in favour of this idea.

It was not until 1935 however that Francois was eventually reunited with her son. According to Jim Barrette: 'She was missing her son and crying all the time so I told her to send for him.' Meanwhile, Con was already 16 years old and unemployed and he welcomed the idea of coming to Trinidad, the land of opportunity.

Con arrived in Trinidad on June 1st 1935, and lived with his mother and her companion Jim Barrette. He was taken by Francois to meet his father, Albert James, then a carpenter also living in Port of Spain. He also met his four brothers and four sisters, the other children of Albert James. After a period of continued unemployment he eventually joined his father's work in carpentry.

Having lived away from each other for so many years, it was not surprising that many difficulties surfaced in the relationship between Elma Francois and her son. Most significantly he had no interest in her politics which seemed to consume so much of her life. Conrad recalls her being arrested or detained from time to time and her accepting it all as a matter of course. She was never interested in dances or 'theatre' (cinema) and only condoned her son's interest in Carnival because he liked it so much himself. After three years he left her home and lived on his own.

Formation of the National Unemployed Movement (NUM)
Elma Francois, Jim Barrette, Jim Headley and later Dudley Mahon were the core group which formed the nucleus of the National Unemployed Movement. Dudley Mahon, a cook at the Port of Spain Colonial Hospital, lived close to Barrette, so they

would meet and talk at the corner of Observatory and Quarry Streets in east Port of Spain. Jim Headley, a Trinidadian, had been based for some years in the United States where he had been a ship's cook. As a seaman he had been active in the radical National Maritime Union and Young Communist League, through which he had come into contact with the Trinidadian George Padmore.

Padmore, born Malcolm Nurse in Tacarigua, was at that time a leading member of the International Trade Union Committee of Negro Workers, a component of the Red International of Labour Unions (RILU). This was created in 1929-1930 in response to the Comintern's recognition of the specific problems of blacks in the United States, the Caribbean and Africa. In 1928 at its Sixth Congress, the Comintern adopted its 'Black-Belt Nation' and Native Republic theses. The monthly periodical of this committee — initially the *International Negro Workers Review*, later renamed the *Negro Worker* — was mailed surreptitiously to Trinidad, according to one writer, within copies of *The Times* of London. This testifies to the importance of seamen in this process. It was this influence of the International Trade Union Committee of Negro Workers (ITCNW) that inspired the major course of direction of the NWCSA when it later emerged.[2]

In 1934, the National Unemployed Movement was formed after a discussion at the home of Headley's mother. Jim Barrette admits his initial scepticism and that of his mother but due to Francois' encouragement he agreed to attend. They discussed the problems of children in Africa, problems such as those illustrated in 'penny pamphlets' which Headley had brought from the United States.

As members of the Trinidad Workingmen's Association, Francois and Headley had sought in vain to encourage Cipriani to pay more attention to the plight of the unemployed. The period 1919-1939 was one of worldwide economic depression. In Trinidad and Tobago this had resulted in a drastic decline in employment among the country's working classes both urban and rural, especially after 1921 and especially among women.

Port of Spain at that time bore telling signs of the depression. Destitutes, many of them Indians, slept in the streets and squares. In fact there were three night shelters for destitute

Indians on Charlotte Street. Africans in the city were mainly servants or 'cabbies' to the Europeans or self-employed traders of some sort. The number of people migrating to the city was growing.

On June 19th 1933, a 'Hunger March' to the Governor in the Red House, the seat of government, took place without the sanction of Cipriani. The marchers demanded the reintroduction of rent-control and relief work. With the formation of the National Unemployed Movement (NUM) in 1934 these 'Hunger Marches' of the unemployed became a regular feature of their activities. This idea spread like wildfire throughout the country and 'Hunger Marches' were organised by other groups.

Some of the most successful of these were the 'Hunger Marches', strikes and disturbances which occurred on the sugar estates in Central Trinidad. Sugar plantation production in Central and South Trinidad still employed large numbers of predominantly Indian workers. The post-war depression, however, and the reorganisation of the production process after 1921, e.g. through mechanisation, had already reduced the number of workers in employment. By the early 1930s contact had been made between the NUM and the sugar workers involved. NUM members for example had been informed by the militant Indian woman sugar worker, Poolbasie, about living and working conditions in the sugar areas, through the customary political meetings which the NWCSA held throughout the country. At these meetings information on local conditions would be exchanged for information on international developments. In addition to the older problems of the sugar belt in the 1930s, the sugar companies sought to pass on the effects of the economic depression to the workers. High unemployment and high rents for barrack accommodation were combined with unilateral increases in the size of tasks — fixed allocations of work to be done. According to Barrette, Poolbasie reported that dishonest drivers were increasingly being sent to check on the completion of tasks and the earth, due to drought, was extremely difficult to work. In addition the practice existed of overseers taking young girls to their bungalows on the pretext that they would 'scrub floors'.

So impressed were NUM members with the militancy of Poolbasie that they dubbed her 'Naidoo' after the Indian Congress

14

Party activist Sarojini Naidoo whose speeches, reported in the pamphlets of the Indian Communists, had greatly impressed them.

These 'Hunger Marches' occurred throughout July 1934. On July 20th, 1934, a march from Caroni and surrounding districts to Port of Spain was planned and arrangements made to meet NUM hunger marchers.

The continuing colonial fear of the unity of African and Indian workers, however, resulted in the march being stopped in Laventille by a 'cordon' of policemen and the Indian sugar workers were prevented from entering the city to meet the predominantly African hunger marchers of the NUM. This however did not prevent the 'Hunger March' fever from spreading. In 1935 during the strike at the Apex Trinidad Oilfields in Fyzabad, Tubal Uriah Buzz Butler made his entry into Trinidad and Tobago labour politics with an abortive 'Hunger March' from South Trinidad to Port of Spain.

In addition to these marches, the NUM also organised a register of unemployed in 1934 and within two weeks 1,200 names were collected in Port of Spain. They used this information in meetings to indicate the extent of unemployment and to convince Cipriani to take this issue more seriously.

By the end of 1934, Headley, victimised and harassed in Trinidad and Tobago, returned to his job as a seaman, but this was not the end of the movement.

Francois' practice of speaking around the town continued to attract members to the organisation. It was in Woodford Square in early 1935 that Bertie Percival, a colleague of T.U.B. Butler in Fyzabad, first heard Francois speak. So impressed was Percival that he introduced himself to her and they discussed the strike then taking place in the Apex oilfields and he was invited to attend a meeting in Quarry Street, Port of Spain. Percival's mother was Vincentian, and although well-educated for that time, he had been refused entrance to a secondary school because his parents had not been married. He had however attended 'training school' paid for by his mother and so would read aloud to her the political books and pamphlets which she would buy but was unable to read.

In 1935 the Trinidadian Rupert Gittens, of Argyle Street in Belmont, returned home from Europe. He had been deported from Marseilles, France, for his activities with the French Communist Party. Mahon and Barrette attended the deportation hearing and Barrette was introduced to Gittens by Mahon.[3]

Under the influence of Gittens the NUM was exposed much more to socialist thinking at an international level and became convinced of the limitations of 'unemployment' as a political issue. At the end of 1935, therefore, the NUM was transformed into the more structured Negro Welfare Cultural and Social Association (NWCSA) at a meeting at the home of Christina King and Bertie Percival in Port of Spain. Percival, in the meantime, had lost his job at the Apex oilfields as a result of the strike.

16

CHAPTER IV
The NWCSA 1935-1936

The new organisation was much more structured and organised than its predecessor. Its activities were divided into four main areas: political work; trade union; cooperative and auxiliary activities; research and education and social work. In the words of Jim Barrette: 'We drew maps and plans of the different villages and read the newspaper on the Public Library Board to identify issues.' Throughout its existence the NWCSA, unlike other contemporary organisations, included a relatively large proportion of women among its membership and they operated effectively at all levels of the organisation.

Throughout her life, Elma Francois was accepted as the chief ideologue of the organisation. In the words of Dudley Mahon, NWCSA member: 'We looked up to her for leadership as she was always right. We had a lot of confidence in her.'[4] Other women members included Christina King who operated as the 'undercover agent' and writer within the organisation. She maintained links with the police, stood bail for imprisoned activists as well as carrying on other organisational activities. King recalls being asked by the infamous Corporal Charlie King: 'Why a nice girl like you bothering with Percival?' Adelaide Harrison was at one time Secretary, while Matilda Goodridge participated mainly in the Social Committee.

This high-level participation of women in the NWCSA was no accident. The fact that a woman, Elma Francois, was its central founding member was a contributory factor. This however was not a sufficient reason.

From its very inception the NWCSA set out to attract women members. It was for this reason the words 'cultural' and 'social' were included in the name of the organisation as these were the areas of work in which, they felt, women could initially be most easily incorporated.

17

Bukka Rennie, in his book *The History of the Working Class in the 20th Century (1919–1956) — The Trinidad and Tobago Experience*, suggests that a definite position on male/female relationships also existed. In his own words, within that organisation:

> The first task of those women who were married was to liberate themselves totally from husband domination, for such domination did in fact forestall the performing of revolutionary duties, especially the duties of cadres which had to be done on a continuous basis.[5]

This was very much reflected in the close, yet autonomous, relationships experienced between members of the organisation. Jim Barrette and Elma Francois lived together and shared a warm, loving and respectful relationship. Christina King, though married to Bertie Percival, maintained the use of her maiden name within the organisation.

The organisation took the position that women and men should cooperate in the development of their collective political consciousness. It rejected the separation of women into 'women's arms' or 'women's auxiliaries'. Within the organisation itself executive positions changed regularly so that these responsibilities were shared among members. The position of Organiser or Organising Secretary, however, was usually the portfolio of Elma Francois.

In 1935 the 'Hunger Marches' of the unemployed continued and, despite Cipriani's attempt, as Mayor of Port of Spain, to ban meetings in Woodford Square, public meetings were held throughout Trinidad and Tobago, and the highlighting of local issues and international issues, such as the arrest of the black U.S. 'Scottsboro boys' and Angelo Herdon, also received attention. Later that year, however, the NWCSA concentrated their activities on action against the invasion of Ethiopia by the Italian fascist Mussolini

The Anti-Abyssinian War Agitation
The importance of the Abyssinian War agitation to the political consciousness of colonial Trinidad and Tobago is yet to be adequately analysed. But the NWCSA was central to this activity. In the words of Dudley Mahon: 'The Abyssinian War

18

awakened the consciousness of the Trinidad working class.'

Ethiopia had a particular significance for the colonised Africans of the New World. It had been the one country to successfully resist European colonising efforts at the end of the 19th century. In addition, its traditional historic links to King Solomon and the Queen of Sheba, popularised through the Garvey movement, made it a symbol of black independence within the entire Caribbean region.

Interest in the war developed within the NWCSA after receiving and reading copies of the *Ethiopian Times* edited by Sylvia Pankhurst, the British socialist feminist and early member of the British Communist Party. The NWCSA also corresponded with Pankhurst, who, through her editorship of her other newspaper *The Dreadnought*, had been in contact with the Jamaican Claude McKay. Small meetings were held throughout the country and the issue caught the interest of large sections of the population. In June–July 1935, headlines such as 'Negroes Awake!' and 'Afro West-Indians be Sincere!' were appearing in the local newspaper *The People* and reflected an increased African race consciousness. One article by Lionel Gill on July 19th 1935, was entitled 'Members of the Black race show your sympathy with Abyssinia — by boycotting all Italian products and Italian merchants doing business in this colony'. That issue also contained a letter to the editor from the NWCSA which was entitled 'Hands off Abyssinia'.

These activities culminated in a mass meeting organised by the NWCSA on the 10th October 1935. 10,000 leaflets were printed and people came to it from every part of the city. At that meeting speakers denounced France for its lukewarm attitude and also denounced England for refusing to sell arms to Ethiopia. They called on all Negroes to boycott French and Italian goods and stevedores were asked to refuse to unload Italian ships. A demonstration marched from the meeting to the office of Seconi, the representative of Italy in Trinidad and Tobago, shouting 'Down with Mussolini!' The meeting unanimously passed two resolutions — the first condemned the 'shooting and bombing of thousands of defenceless men, women and children for the purpose of glorifying Italian Fascist Imperialism', while the second 'criticised the prohibition of meetings and marches as a direct attack upon the

19

political rights of the working class by a government incompetent to solve the unemployment crisis'.[6] Thus the link was made between local and international political developments.

The response to this meeting was tremendous. Local black Roman Catholics wrote letters of support for the campaign to the press and expressed disappointment with the Pope's blessing of the Italian troops. This was further stimulated by a statement of one Christopher Percival to the Roman Catholic Archbishop of Trinidad and Tobago, critical of the Church's position.

Among middle-class Afro-Trinidadians an emotional feeling of racial solidarity and accompanying action were also evident. Letters of congratulation were sent to the NWCSA by the McShine brothers and an organisation — the Friends of Ethiopia Committee — was formed to which Elma Francois and Bertie Percival, as representatives of the NWCSA, were invited to speak. Their resolution on Ethiopia, taken to the meeting, was accepted without change.

Other organisations emerged during this period. The United Negro Improvement Association (UNIA), Marcus Garvey's organisation, was revitalised. The Daughters of Ethiopia, a grouping of women, concentrated on fund-raising for Ethiopia through such activities as the sale of red, black and green flags and musical evenings. Others included the Afro-West Indian League, the West Indian Youth Welfare League, Brotherhood and African Progeny and the African National High School of 25 Park Street, Port of Spain, whose courses included African languages. In December 1935, *The People* reported that a Catholic Church bazaar in La Brea was not supported because of the dissatisfaction felt by the parishioners with the Pope's position on Ethiopia.

There was an upsurge in this agitation again in May 1936 as it became evident, by that time, that Britain had retreated from any solution based on effective sanctions or force to one based on negotiations between Italy and Ethiopia. The Italians, therefore, gained an empire and Haile Selassie began his five-year exile. According to Robert G. Weisbord: 'The worst fears of the West Indians had been realised.' On Saturday 9th May a large crowd at a Friends of Ethiopia meeting endorsed a plea for Britain to assist Abyssinia at the Peace

20

Talks. Later that month, on Friday 29th May, the NWCSA held a mass meeting in Woodford Square. Elma Francois was the main speaker and spoke on the attitude of the League of Nations, noting that Ethiopia had loyally observed the covenant of the League. She also denounced the barbaric methods used by Italy against an innocent and defenceless black people.

The Italian invasion of Ethiopia engaged the minds and awoke the solidarity of the people of Trinidad and Tobago in a way that few issues have since then. The NWCSA were particularly instrumental in bringing this to the consciousness of people throughout the country and in moving them to action. And Elma Francois had been the spearhead.

Struggle Against Cipriani

The importance of Arthur Andrew Cipriani in the history of the working class of Trinidad and Tobago cannot be denied. His struggles for basic rights for workers such as the eight-hour day, workmen's compensation, and a trade union ordinance laid the basis for gains made by the labour movement in later years. Most students of labour history however will admit that Cipriani was handicapped by three major factors:

1. His class position as a landowner from the propertied Catholic French Creole class often presented him with serious conflicts of interest in his activities.

2. His almost complete acceptance of the British Labour Party brand of 'Labour and Socialism' and his adherence to their priorities and policies as a yardstick by which to measure developments in Trinidad and Tobago.

3. His discouragement of popular working-class participation in struggles in their own interests, and in its place putting himself forward as their spokesman who would negotiate on their behalf.

In addition to these three factors, which characterised the overall career of Cipriani, by the early 1930s his recurring election as Mayor of the Port of Spain City Council often placed him in dispute with those very groups that he claimed to represent. The main distinction between the approach of the NWCSA and that of Cipriani to issues in general was on the issue of autonomous working-class organisation. While

21

the NWCSA saw the need for workers to organise themselves in their own interest, Cipriani sought to maintain their dependence on his negotiations with the 'better classes'.

Elma Francois' criticism of Cipriani, as mentioned earlier, began when she was still a member of the TWA. As the NWCSA criticism of him increased, Cipriani was able to use his increasing powers against them. On May Day 1935, for example, Cipriani as a member of the City Council decided to highlight the Council's attempt, since 1928, to take over the electric and tramway franchise from the foreign-owned Trinidad Electric Company. In a counter meeting the NWCSA, while supporting the issue, called for more decisive action to bring about a conclusion. At this meeting, Elma Francois made her most famous criticism of Cipriani referring to him as 'Britain's best policeman in the colonies',[7] and the meeting ended up with the made-up chorus:

> We will hang Cipriani on the sour apple tree
> When the red revolution comes.[8]

Supporters of the TWA marched up to the Transfer Station after the meeting, and attempted to dig up rails and overturn tramcars. In the words of the *Trinidad Guardian* of 9th May, 1935:

> While Cipriani told in deliberate tones the outcome of his efforts, news came that the tramrails were being dug up on Frederick Street near to the Town Hall. This necessitated a hold up of No. 5 St. Clair car, the passengers of which had to alight.

As early as August 1935 Cipriani had sought to prevent the NWCSA from using Woodford Square for its political meetings. In 1936, with the increase in their activity, his efforts to prevent the NWCSA using Woodford Square also increased. Throughout the NWCSA's existence, however, its main area of activity was 'The Greens' on Piccadilly Street, a small patch of green grass where small public meetings were held.

Between 1935 and 1936 links were established with T.U.B. Butler through Bertie Percival. Percival had participated with Butler in the 1935 strike at Apex oilfields and had allowed him to stay at his home in East Port of Spain while Percival wrote letters seeking compensation for the injured Butler.

22

The NWCSA accepted the necessity to work with Butler, another former TLP member, largely because of his great success in mobilising workers primarily in Point Fortin and Fyzabad. Grave differences however existed between them and Butler, and Elma Francois, in particular, often voiced her disapproval. The two main bones of contention with Butler were: Butler's loyalty to the British throne and the relevance of religion to political struggle.

In May 1936, for example, when the NWCSA called on the people to denounce the British as imperialists if they wanted to show solidarity with the people of the African continent, Butler's approach was to call on people to support Britain against Mussolini.[9] On the issue of religion Francois, a non-believer, decried the hold which religion had over the lives of poor people. Making no secret of her view, Francois nevertheless used her deep knowledge of the Bible to argue and discuss with people. In the words of Barrette 'she used the Bible like a little walking-stick'.[10]

To some extent Butler, like Cipriani, saw the solution to the problems of the working class in the extension of the full rights of British citizens to all. This was reflected in the name later given to his organisation — the British Empire Workers and Citizens Home Rule Party. At the same time his method of mobilisation was strongly religious. His Butler Moravian Baptist Church served as both a social and financial base for his activities and, some suggest, an appropriate venue to attract his many female supporters.

Francois' approach to religion, therefore, evoked strong feelings from some, including many of Butler's predominantly women supporters. The NWCSA, and especially Francois, were derided for their anti-religious position and referred to as the 'Godless Horde'. In spite of this, however, the NWCSA continued to cooperate with Butler as the working-class catalyst of the developing labour movement.

The Cost of Living Issue
As noted earlier NWCSA activities concentrated a great deal on the improvement of the quality of life of the country's working-class people, many of whom earned next to nothing

or were unemployed during the inter-war depression. In 1936 much emphasis was given to these activities.

One issue taken up was the cost of condensed milk, at that time a staple in the working-class diet. To press their case a Condensed Milk Association was registered in 1936 under the Trade Union Ordinance, one of the first organisations to do so.

Household consumption was one area where the NWCSA did not question the sexual division of labour. A delegation comprising mostly women members visited the importers T. Geddes Grant and Co. Ltd. They raised the question of price differences for two brands of condensed milk and the propaganda which forced members to buy the more expensive brand for their babies. On the sexual composition of the delegation, Jim Barrette had this to say:

> We did it that way because the woman is the head of the house, not the man, when it coming to goods, they does buy, not the man.[11]

Based on concerns such as these, it was decided to send a high-powered delegation to visit the then Governor, Sir Murchison Fletcher. The visit was arranged by Colonial Secretary Howard Nankivell, who maintained clandestine relations with the NWCSA and was eventually recalled from Trinidad and Tobago in 1937 for his apparent support for the cause of the strikers.

In preparing their memorandum much research went into the cost of living, nutritional standards, hospital services, old age pension, school meals and health services. They also held discussions with organisations such as the Clerks Union, the Amalgamated Building and Woodworkers Union, representatives of the persecuted Spiritual Baptists and other labour movement activists.

In the actual delegation, Jim Barrette, then NWCSA president, was asked to step down in favour of T.U.B. Butler for the sake of unity and organisational representativeness. Elma Francois, who was leader of the delegation, objected strenuously to this but accepted the will of the majority.

The historic meeting with the Governor, Sir Murchison Fletcher, took place on Tuesday November 8th, 1936, and

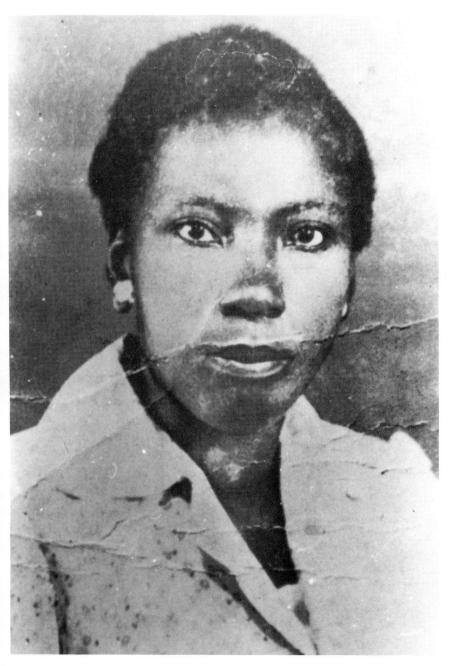

Elma Francois

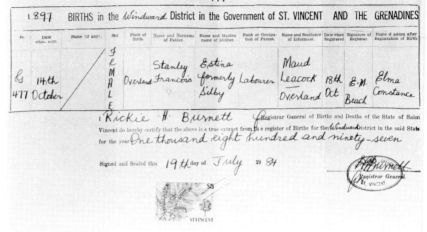

PAGE 474

1897 BIRTHS in the *Windward* District in the Government of ST. VINCENT AND THE GRENADINES

No.	Date when born	Name (if any)	Sex	Place of Birth	Name and Surname of Father	Name and Maiden name of Mother	Rank or Occupation of Parent	Name and Residence of Informant	Date when Registered	Signature of Registrar	Name if added after Registration of Birth
6 477	14th October		FEMALE	Overland	Stanley Francois	Estina formerly Silby	Labourer	Maud Leacock — Overland	18th Oct	E.M. Beach	Elma Constance

I *Rickie H. Burnett* Registrar General of Births and Deaths of the State of Saint Vincent do hereby certify that the above is a true extract from the e register of Births for the *Windward* District in the said State for the year *One thousand eight hundred and ninety-seven*

Signed and Sealed this *19th* day of *July* 19 *84*

Registrar General ST. VINCENT

The birth certificate of Elma Francois

Cotton ginnery in St Vincent at the turn of the century

Conrad James, son of Elma Francois, in Cairo, Egypt, 1945

Christina King and Bertie Percival in the 1930s, taken from *Glory Dead* by Arthur Calder Marshall

Jim Barrette

T.U.B. Butler in an earlier period (OWTU library)

Jim Barrette in 1985

Christina King in 1985

Jim Barrette and Christina King talking with the author, Rhoda
Reddock, in their home in 1985

GAIETY

Wednesday 8th at 5 p.m. only. Ladies Matinee
DOUBLE   PROGRAMME

1. CLEOPATRA with Warren William and Claudette Colbert
2. TOO MUCH HARMONY with Bing Crosby

Usual Ladies Matinee Prices

Wednesday 8th at 8.30 p.m.   Popular Ladies Night
DOUBLE   ATTRACTION

1. Grand Farewell Calypso Show

With RADIO, TIGER, INVADER and others

Come and hear the leading Calypsonians in their best numbers before they leave the island on a tour of the West Indies.

Main Topic:
THE BOROUGH COUNCILLORS AND PAY

With RADIO representing the Burgesses and TIGER the Councillors Don't fail to come to the GAIETY and hear the decision. Also:-

1. *POWER OF THE WOMEN OF TRINIDAD*
2. *SHOP HOURS CLOSING ORDINANCE*
3. *THE JEW IMMIGRATION—Tiger*
4. *IS RHYTHM WE WANT—Radio*

and many other items including **WAR !**

Picture : **CLEOPATRA** with Claudette Colbert

Prices : 8, 12, 18c. Ladies 8c except in Bal.

Thurs. 9th at 5 p.m. also Friday at 5 & 8.30 Daily

'Her Jungle Love'

USUAL MID-WEEK PRICES

SAT. AT 9.30 MATINEE

1. **NEVADA** with BUSTER CRABBE

2. **Tonight Is Ours.**

Starting Sunday

Again we venture to Guarantee another Double. 2 Weekend Pictures for one Weekend.

1. College Holiday
2. THE GREAT GAMBINI

USUAL WEEK-END PRICES.

A cinema publicity bill, which includes a reference to the Shop Hours Closing Ordinance

for the first time in the history of Trinidad and Tobago, the delegation included a large proportion of women. In fact according to Barrette, the initial response of one member of the government team was 'What am I seeing, West Indian women on a political delegation?' But before the women, including Francois, could have an opportunity to put forward their well-prepared memorandum T.U.B. Butler took over the event's proceedings. First he fell on his knees, kissed the Governor's hand and begged for his assistance paying little heed to the prepared statement for the duration of the meeting.[12]

In a report of this meeting given at Emporium Hall, Fyzabad, on December 13th, 1936, Butler praised 'Friend Fletcher' whom he reported had promised justice and fairplay and equal courtesy to one and all as well as the scrapping of the Shop Hours Committee's recommendations, which will be discussed later.[13]

The NWCSA members understandably were not so pleased with the outcome, in particular Francois who had warned of such an eventuality. Later on after the 1937 disturbances, Fletcher was to report that the NWCSA had been the first organisation to bring to his attention the conditions of life in the country.

In another attempt to improve the living conditions of the poor, the NWCSA sought to open access to the Bruce Stephens Trust Fund. This was a fund that had been established, on the death of Stephens, a local white, for the needy of Port of Spain. This fund, however, was monopolised by the less well-to-do whites for private education. In 1936, the NWCSA sought to open up access to the fund to all the poor and suffering of Port of Spain, who were faced with the daily realities around them in the 'John-John' area of Port of Spain. NWCSA members were accused of being paid by the persons whom they brought for relief. So on one occasion Percival was arrested by Inspector Liddelow, but the crowd of people however stood before Liddelow denying that they had been paid to come there. A demonstration which went to the Fund's headquarters attracted thousands of the suffering but they were met by police including Corporal Charlie King, who was later to be burnt alive by a crowd after attempting to arrest Butler on June 19, 1937.

After Percival's arrest and self-defence in court, the Fund was investigated and opened up to the destitute, unemployed and bed-ridden of Port of Spain for whom it had been originally intended.

The NWCSA also showed its concern with the daily living conditions of the people in the social welfare activities of the organisation. Social work in the first half of this century was an important means of gaining prestige for oneself or one's group. Originally the preserve of ladies of the European plantocracy and colonial bureaucratic class, other groups accepted this as a means of gaining recognition and support in the community. This concern for issues of day-to-day survival as well as overall rights and anti-colonial struggle characterised the work of the NWCSA throughout its existence.

The Shop Hours Agitation
By far the most significant activity of 1936 however, in the eyes of NWCSA members, was the agitation against the Shop Hours (Opening and Closing) Bill.

In December 1921, the Shop Hours Ordinance had been passed after much agitation by shop assistants and clerks. It gave a 45-hour week to shop assistants and clerks in dry goods shops, wholesale provision shops, hardware, jewellery and pawnbrokers' shops as well as stationers and booksellers. These new hours were from 8.00 a.m. to 4.00 p.m. on five days and 8.00 a.m. to 1.00 p.m. on the sixth. Genuine 'small stores' were exempted from the order.

In 1929, this Ordinance was extended to define 'small stores' as those in which one proprietor and not more than two persons were engaged. These could open from 7.00 a.m. to 7.00 p.m. on weekdays and up to 8.00 p.m. on Saturdays.

In June 1936, a new Bill, the Shop Hours (Closing and Opening) Bill,[14] was introduced in response to pressure from merchants, in particular those represented by the Chamber of Commerce. This Bill sought to remove this 'advantage' (according to the businessmen) which small (predominantly non-white) shopkeepers had of longer opening hours.

26

The NWCSA took up this issue on behalf of the small shopkeepers and held mass meetings throughout the country. *The People* newspaper of June-July reported on this issue and included letters to the editor from as far away as Fyzabad. At a mass meeting in Woodford Square on June 25th 1936, 600 workers present passed a resolution against the Ordinance. In July, however, Cipriani refused the NWCSA permission to hold a meeting on the Shop Hours issue at Woodford Square. But by November Cipriani was replaced by Port of Spain druggist, Alfred Richards, as Mayor of Port of Spain, and his attitude to the organisation was more favourable than Cipriani's.

Between late 1936 and early 1938 the attention of the NWCSA was diverted away from this issue, and with good reason as will be seen later. It was taken up again in 1938.

By the end of 1936, the influence of the NWCSA had begun to be felt within the country. Prior to the visit to the colonial Governor, Murchison Fletcher, T.U.B. Butler had been a nominal member of the NWCSA, but in August 1936 he formed his own British Empire Workers and Citizen's Home Rule Party (BEW&CHRP). In spite of disagreements, the NWCSA continued to support Butler's activities in the south as a complement to their own activities in the north. The proletarian intellectuals in the NWCSA never had the mass appeal that Butler developed.

CHAPTER V
The NWCSA 1937-1939

The year 1937 saw a concentration of NWCSA activities on workers struggles and the development of the emerging trade union movement.

As noted earlier, after years of agitation by Cipriani, the Trade Union Ordinance was passed in 1932. This Ordinance however, unlike the British Act of Parliament on trade unions, did not give legal protection to peaceful picketing or exemption from legal actions for damages arising from strike action. As a result of this, based on the advice of the British Labour Party, Cipriani refused to register the TWA as a trade union, nor did he advise the affiliated Clerks Union and Stevedores Union to do so.

At that time Elma Francois and Jim Headley were still TWA members. In contrast, they advised that the unions should register and then fight to make changes and improvements in the Ordinance. By 1937, therefore, at a time when workers were suffering the effects of the inter-war depression — unemployment, high cost of living, job insecurity and racism from employers — they had little real recourse to redress their conditions. Only one trade union, the Amalgamated Building and Woodcutters Union, was registered before 1937.

The effects of this constellation of factors had already brought matters to a head in the sugar estates of Central Trinidad in 1934 and at Apex oilfields in Fyzabad in 1935. In 1937 the wage labourers in South Trinidad were restless.

The events of June 1937 have been well documented and there is no need to go into them here. What is less well known is the relationship of Francois and other NWCSA members to these events.

The NWCSA and the Events of 1937

There can be no dispute about the fact that the figure of Tubal Uriah Buzz Butler dominated the scene during the events of June 1937 and for much of the time thereafter. What is interesting to note however is the continuation of political action and resistance after his 'disappearance' on June 19th 1937, and during his subsequent internment on Nelson Island after September 1937.

Among those 'keeping the fires burning', not unexpectedly, was the NWCSA. In his book, Rennie suggests that plans for a joint strike between the north and south scheduled for June 21st were thwarted as the authorities became informed about it.[15] This suggestion is supported by a report in *The People* of June 19th, 1937, which noted that a mass meeting planned by the NWCSA in Port of Spain on Thursday 18th was postponed after a letter of protest from certain councillors and aldermen to the town clerk. The protest letter denounced the circular advertising the meeting as 'not only libellous, but of an inflammatory character and as such might lead to disorder'.[16]

The developments of June 19th, however, took the NWCSA members based in the north by surprise. Conrad James, son of Elma Francois, recalls his mother awakening him at 3.00 a.m. in the morning of the 20th, saying that there were riots in Fyzabad, Charlie King had been burned and she was leaving immediately for Fyzabad. His attempts to discourage her from leaving were useless. Francois spent the following day in Fyzabad investigating everything and returned to Port of Spain in the evening.[17]

The very next day, June 21st 1937, on the instigation of Francois, the NWCSA went into action in North Trinidad. On the 22nd June the *Trinidad Guardian* reported on page one 'City Strike, One Wounded'. It noted that the first strike occurred among labourers, carpenters and masons working on the new Treasury Building. They were joined by a 'band of men' from the Negro Welfare Cultural and Social Association who proceeded to the Trinidad Trading Company and the Harbour Scheme Works and ordered the employees to cease work. While most research has concentrated on activities in the south, significant strike and protest activity also occurred in the north of the country. Soon 'All Stores [were] closed in Port of Spain',[18] as the strike spread to Belmont, St. James and Woodbrook. Schools were given a half-holiday and even small stores and coal shops were closed as looting broke out in the evening.

By June 23rd when the *Guardian* reported 'Strike Spell Broken in San Fernando', it also noted the following: 'Strike Fever in Arima', 'Demonstration on Sugar Estates' — in Orange Grove, in St. Augustine — and a 'Sit-down sympathy strike at the Government Farm and St. Augustine Experimental Station'.

By the 24th, strikes were reported in Blanchisseuse, at the Bamboo Paper Pulp factory in Champs Fleurs, Trinidad Clay Products and Aranguez Estates in Aranguez, San Juan. In an article headlined 'Strike Moves Fast' the *Guardian* of June 25th, 1937 reported:

> Men, young and old, women and children brandishing sticks, cutlasses and other weapons walked from factory to factory in the district, inflicting workers with the strike fever...

Throughout this period virtually all groups of labourers went on strike. City scavengers' and bus drivers' strike action compounded the situation. By June 28th the NWCSA members — Elma Francois, Caesar Ashby, Jim Barrette and Bertie Percival — were arrested and spent seven days in jail. One member, Dudley Mahon, was not arrested and so organised their defence through the Guyanese lawyer, E.P. Bruyning, who defended NWCSA members on many occasions. On this occasion their defence cost $35.00.

The case against Bertie Percival was the most clearly false as he, like Christopher Harper, had been in Fyzabad with Butler at the time of the alleged 'unlawful assembly' on June 22nd in Port of Spain.[19] He was acquitted on the counter evidence of Timothy Roodal and news reporter Charles Eversley. The trial of Barrette, Ashby and Francois was put off to July 19th and they were eventually acquitted.

At this trial their positions in the NWCSA were identified as: Ashby, Chairman; Barrette, Organiser; Percival, Assistant

Organiser and Elma Francois, Education Directress. Christina King, meanwhile, was active in the south with Percival and Harper.

In spite of the charges, NWCSA members continued the mobilisation throughout the year 1937. Meetings were held in the north and south including Fyzabad, Point Fortin and Siparia, partly under the auspices of the Workers Defence Committee formed in conjunction with members of Butler's British Empire Workers and Citizens Home Rule Party (BEW&CHRP). In addition to collecting funds for legal defence and for assistance to the children of the imprisoned, they also circulated confused reports on Butler's whereabouts.

On September 27th 1937, Butler was arrested as he went to give evidence before the Labour Disturbances Commission, more commonly known as the Forster Commission, sent by the Colonial Office in England to 'enquire into' the causes of the disturbances.

In response to this action by the authorities, on Tuesday 28th September a meeting on Reclaimed Lands, South Quay, passed a resolution demanding Butler's release. Thereafter meetings were held throughout 'Leaseholds', Palo Seco and in Siparia calling on oil workers to press for the withdrawal of all charges against Butler. It is interesting to note that in spite of personal and political differences between the NWCSA and Butler, these were put aside in the wider class interest. At the meetings Jim Barrette warned that a second general strike would result if Butler were jailed and amidst great harassment the meetings continued.

Disapproval of these activities came not only from the colonial authorities but also from Oilfields Workers Trade Union (OWTU) officials A.C. Rienzi and E.R. Blades who, in late September, signed a statement condemning what they saw to be a strike call but pledging to give Butler 'every moral assistance to enable him to be properly defended'.[20] It was at one of these meetings in Siparia that Jim Barrette was arrested and jailed, and then transferred to Port of Spain. Along with his comrades Bertie Percival and Alexander Duke he was accused of having distributed seditious pamphlets.

It is important to note here that NWCSA activities in 1937 were not limited to Trinidad and Tobago. NWCSA member

Clement Payne, son of a Barbadian father and Trinidadian mother, was a key mobiliser in the 1937 disturbances in Barbados, for which he was deported. The NWCSA was aware of their larger Caribbean and their general international responsibilities.

The Sedition Trials 1937-1938
Between 1937 and 1938 NWCSA members were faced with sedition charges arising out of the labour disturbances of June 1937. These trials were important and significant in that they adversely affected the support base of the organisation. NWCSA members continued to work among the people and within the labour movement but people were made to feel more afraid and told of the danger that may arise from their association with the NWCSA.

In October 1937, the *Trinidad Guardian* reported that the Port of Spain City Council and the Government had agreed to cooperate in refusing to grant permission to any organisation likely 'to hold meetings of a seditious or scurrilous nature' in any of the public squares or parks of the city. Special reference was made to trade union leaders.

In the debate on the issue in the City Council, not all the members of the Council were unanimous in their support of the colonial government's suggestion. Councillors Lai-Fook, Garnet McCarthy and Audrey Jeffers argued against the suggestion but in the end conceded to a motion agreeing to cooperate with the government.

That same month, on October 13th, the NWCSA members Jim Barrette, Bertie Percival and Alexander Duke were tried at the Siparia Magistrates Court, charged with having distributed seditious pamphlets in the oil belt at Fyzabad and Palo Seco in September 1937. The pamphlets had called for an end to plans for deportation and for Uriah Butler to be freed. Percival had previously been convicted in June 1936 for assault and battery, in April 1937 for disorderly behaviour and in June 1937 for using violent language. Such was the persecution suffered by NWCSA members.

In this case, in October 1937, Percival was convicted and put on a $100 bond for good behaviour for one year. Alexander Duke was acquitted and also put on a $100 bond.

Jim Barrette was convicted and given a four-month suspended sentence. He admitted to distributing the pamphlets but not to their seditious nature. He gave notice of his intention to appeal. On July 18th Barrette had already been put on a personal bond in Port of Spain for taking part in an unlawful assembly on St. Vincent Street on June 22nd.

Later that year, Barrette, with the support of progressive lawyers of the day, won his appeal. In immediate response to this, a bill was introduced into the Legislative Council to replace trial by jury with trial by three state-appointed judges. This proposal was fought legally with the help of lawyers, such as L.C. Hannays, and numerous letters to the press called for the sedition cases to be tried by jury. As a result of this opposition the Bill was not re-introduced.

In February 1938 a much more serious set of sedition trials of NWCSA members began. The first of these was of Bertie Percival, Elma Francois and Darlington Marshall, who was not a member of the NWCSA. They were all charged and tried in separate trials for 'uttering words having a seditious intention'. For both Francois and Percival the charges referred to a public meeting on 'The Greens' on Piccadilly Street, Port of Spain on October 13, 1937. In the words of her colleague Christina King:

> After Jim was freed in the country, Francois was so tired she only wanted to go home and cook some fish. The night before she had given a speech in defence of Jim. Before she could get home properly, she and Bertie Percival were arrested for sedition from these speeches...

Darlington Marshall was charged with the same offence of 'uttering words having a seditious intention'. He had spoken at a meeting on 'The Greens' on the 30th September 1937. The topic of the meeting was 'getting Butler freed'.[21] Marshall, a follower of Butler, was incorrectly accused of being a member of the NWCSA, most likely because of the working relationship, though difficult at times, which existed between the two organisations.

The Elma Francois Sedition Trial
The central trial in all these cases was that of Elma Francois. In February 1938 Francois became the first woman in the

history of Trinidad and Tobago to be tried for sedition.

The trial began on the 14th February 1938, at the second Port of Spain Assize Court before Justice A.C. Robinson, who had also presided over the other sedition trials. Appearing on her behalf was lawyer E.P. Bruyning. Prosecutor in the case was Acting Solicitor General Mr. C.T.W.E. Worrell.

The jury, as was normal in those days, was all-male and was drawn from those classes which met the property and other qualifications for jury service at the time.

Witnesses used in the case, as in all the sedition cases, were police officers. In this case the witnesses were Detective Sergeant Henry Maxime and Super-Sergeant Caesar. These police officers usually attended the political meetings in 'plainclothes' and either took shorthand notes or wrote 'verbatim' reports *after* having left the political meetings.

Francois, unlike the other defendants, undertook the greater part of her own defence herself — against the advice of barrister E.P. Bruyning who preferred to speak on behalf of all. She had faced another charge earlier for taking part in a procession in Port of Spain but that case had been dismissed.

In outlining the case, C.T.W.E. Worrell advised the jury to consider whether the language used by the defendant was such that ought to be used in the circumstances of general unrest in the colony. According to the *Trinidad Guardian* of February 15th, he concluded his indictment by noting that:

It was perhaps unnecessary for him to ask them to deal with the accused woman on the merits of the case and not with regard to her being a woman at all.

He did not think that would make things any easier for her because he believed with Kipling that the female of the species was more deadly than the male.

The first witness, Sergeant Henry Maxime, reported on the meeting held on October 13th 1937, at 'The Greens' on Piccadilly Street. There were about 150 persons present, 'persons in the ordinary walk of life mostly from the labouring classes'. According to Maxime, Francois had dealt with the sedition cases of Barrette and Percival which had been tried in Siparia that morning, stating that:

34

They are framed up charges of Colonial Imperialism to strike terror-ism into the hearts of the Negro and East Indian workers. The more prosecutions, the more jail sentences, the more ill-treatment of the workers by the police is the more hatred the workers will have for a British Colonial Imperialism. In the West Indies, the moment you say strike you get jail sentences because you are Negro and East Indian workers: but in England and all over the world, the strike is a common thing.

There are strikes in England almost weekly. The workers of the Soviet Republic get equal privileges and obtain better conditions. In Trinidad when the workers ask for bread they get bullets and jail-sentences.... [22]

According to the witness she had made reference in continuing her speech to evidence put before the Labour Disturbances Commission, then in the country, about how an innocent by-stander was fired upon by a military volunteer. Apparently Francois had also used this opportunity to launch her campaign against local participation in or support for the upcoming World War II. According to Sergeant Maxime's notes she had stated:

This is what we get for asking for bread — bullets: but war clouds are now hanging over Europe and political howlers will soon be coming to ask you, the same people who when you ask for bread are shot like dogs and given jail sentences, to fight for them. But we will tell them that we will not fight in any war. The only war we will fight is in the fight to better conditions, peace and liberty.

After defence lawyer E.P. Bruyning's cross-examination Elma Francois herself entered the witness box and delivered her stirring self-defence. This has been reproduced previously and is here given again in full.

Elma Francois' Speech in her Self-Defence at her Sedition Trial
'I am one of the Negro Welfare Cultural and Social Association. The Association was formed about 4 years ago. I am one of the founders. My occupation is clothes-washing. The aims and objectives of the Association are:

1. To struggle for the development and better welfare of the Negro people.
2. To develop solidarity with the oppressed Negro people of the West Indies and the entire world.

35

3. To make known the conditions of the oppressed Negro people and their struggle against oppression.

4. To win the masses of oppressed people the world over in a struggle for the better welfare of the Negro people.

'In keeping with the aims and objectives of our Association, we hold meetings. I keep in touch with local affairs, I follow the local politics as best I can. We particularly pay attention to the underdog.

'My organisation expects to achieve our aims and objectives by sending in protest resolutions, petitions and delegations. This is part of my method to achieve my aims. I do not hope to achieve them by violence. We denounce violence at every meeting. On the night of October 13, 1937, we held a meeting on the "Greens" on Piccadilly Street.

'There were three speakers, Bertie Percival, Comrade Peters and myself. We always elected a chairman before going to a meeting. Our meetings are well planned beforehand and we would decide on a chairman. Comrade Percival was chairman that night. I arranged beforehand what subject my address would be based on. The subject of my address was "World Imperialism and the Colonial Toilers". The chairman announced the subject and then I commenced. In dealing with my subject I dealt with world conditions linking them up with local conditions; I dealt with land reservations in the Kenya Colony. I explained that a certain amount of land was reserved for the working class and often they were deprived of it and they decided there to organise in order to get their wrongs righted with regard to the question of land reservations, by a Royal Commission. They succeeded in getting a Royal Commission.

'I dealt with Nigeria. I dealt with the natives there protesting against increased taxations. I further told them that only by organised unity can we gain better conditions. I discussed Germany and Russia also. I pointed out the effective method the workers in England used by organising and what they gained. I spoke about the Negro and East-Indian workers who sleep under the Town Hall and in the Square through poverty. I wanted their conditions to be bettered. I referred to the struggle my organisation had carried out against the Trade

36

Tax. We sent out a resolution and carried out an island-wide campaign and we collected hundreds of signatures and forwarded them by way of petition to the Governor Claude Hollis. The Tax has since been removed. I then dealt with the Shop Closing Ordinance. My organisation sent a petition with thousands of signatures also to Governor Murchison Fletcher. I produced a copy of the petition. My organisation sent a delegation to Fletcher on the unemployed question. I led the delegation. I handed him a copy of our demands.

'I made an appeal to my audience to assist us financially in aid of the arrested workers. I also reminded them of the charge against Comrade Percival at the "Greens" on the night of the 13th. I was dealing with terror in Germany under the fascist Government and I said that hundreds of workers were being placed in jail. I said that jail sentences and executions do not solve our problems. It is only by organised unity can we better conditions. I discussed the conditions in Soviet Russia. I said workers of the world were not prepared to fight in any way but for bread, peace and liberty.'

She was asked by the Court to define 'World Imperialism and Colonialism'. She described the relationship between the ruling classes of the world and the exploited workers of the colonies. And when asked what German workers had to do with her, she replied that they meant something to her as a worker. During cross-examination she was asked by the prosecutor, Mr C.T.W.E. Worrell, why she persisted in making speeches which were 'causing disaffection among his Majesty's subjects'. To this she replied indignantly:

'I don't know that my speeches create disaffection, I know that my speeches create a fire in the minds of the people so as to change the conditions which now exist, and it isn't for me here to tell you what is existing because I believe that you are a son of some working-class family despite your lofty position as you stand before me as a prosecutor.'

After making her statement Francois faced the cross-examination of C.T.W.E. Worrell and on being asked she identified her occupation as clothes-washer. He continued in the following manner, a good illustration of the approach to women political activists:

'When last did you wash clothes?

— Up to Sunday.
— That is your own bed linen, I suppose.
— No, clothes.
— What clothes?
— Male clothes.
— I'll bet they were Bertie Percival's clothes?
— No.
— That is your occupation?
— Yes.
— And the Association is your pastime?
— No.
— What is it, a hobby?
— I consider it an organisation in the interests of the working classes.'[23]

On the third day of the trial, after hearing the judge's summing up, the jury came to a unanimous verdict of 'not guilty' and Francois was discharged.

The sedition trials of 1937/38 had a strong negative effect on the organisation, as had no doubt been the intention of the colonial state. In fact, on the first day of her trial, Francois had mentioned being informed by a police officer that they were out to destroy the Association.

This, however, was not the end. The members rallied on against the great odds. Arthur Calder-Marshall, both in his memorandum to the 1938 West India Royal Commission and in his book *Glory Dead*, reported on a public meeting of the NWCSA in Woodford Square. About 250 people were grouped around. Francois was speaking on the Shop Hours Bill. According to Calder-Marshall she called on the crowd to listen carefully to what she was saying so that when (not if) they were arrested they could depend on them to testify on their behalf. She continued:

> I am not appealing for violence, I do not want you to resort to force. But I do implore you to protest against the Shop Hours Bills, I implore you to sign the protest and make your friends sign it. Then we will present it to the Governor.[24]

The meeting was eventually broken up by a white police inspector and a detective. In response, Francois, Percival and Christina King proceeded to sing the Internationale standing

38

MASS MEETING

TO-NIGHT

THURSDAY 7TH JULY 1938, AT 7.30 P.M. SHARP

at 66 George Street

Renewal of Protest Shop Hours Ordinance Bill.

THE WORKING CLASSES OF ALL COUNTRIES PRO-
TEST AGAINST ANY ATTACK THAT TENDS TO
REDUCE THEIR LIVING STANDARD TO ONE OF
MISERY, STARVATION, AND DEATH.

THE RECENT SHOP HOURS BILL THAT HAS BEEN
PASSED BY THE LEGISLATIVE COUNCIL, IF
PUT INTO EFFECT WILL BRING IN ITS
TRAIN INTOLERABLE HARDSHIP ON THE
TOILING MASSES OF THIS COUNTRY.

The Pretended Pretext of this Bill, if such Talk of Protecting the Clerk is True

Come TO-NIGHT and Hear FRANCOIS, PERCIVAL, and PAYNE.

Outstanding Negro Leaders.—The N. W. Cul. & Social Assoc.

SUPPORT THE NEGRO WELFARE CULTURAL
AND SOCIAL ASSOCIATION

For Better Living Conditions

JOIN NOW

on the grass with their heads raised. Apparently permission for the meeting had been requested from the Mayor, both verbally and in writing, but in spite of these attempts they had got no reply.

This meeting, discussed here, occurred during the period when Barrette was imprisoned for distributing seditious pamphlets in Siparia. Calder-Marshall captures the situation in the following words:

> Francoise [sic] was more emotional. She had been working all day and every day for the appeal of Jim Barrette ... Francois was almost starving. But her devotion to Barrette engrossed her. She did not spare herself, going from place to place for funds for his appeal ...
>
> She was so desperate because the fire in her was so strong that she could not understand the indifference that would leave a leader to suffer for this leadership...
>
> 'If it hadn't been for Comrade Barrette,' she said to me, 'I would have made them arrest me and put me behind bars. We, all of us would.' She was tired, exhausted by the struggle.[25]

Sedition trials of other NWCSA members continued in early 1938. This time Jim Barrette was imprisoned for nine months. *The People* of 14th May 1938 reported that when the May Day demonstration passed the jail, Jim Barrette could be heard joining in the singing of the Internationale. So loud was his intervention that the prison warden asked him to lower his voice. At these May Day celebrations the plans for an appeal to the Privy Council on his behalf were announced.[26]

The sedition trials of 1937/38 are a clear reflection of the fear felt by the authorities for the potential and influence of the NWCSA. After having experienced the effects of working-class self-action they were loath to allow it to happen again. The fact is however that these trials and convictions did not daunt the members of the NWCSA. They simply took the trials in their stride and moved on to the next issue.

The Continuation of the Shop Hours Bill Agitation

In early 1938 agitation against the Shop Hours (Opening and Closing) Bill surfaced again, and on Friday, 6th May, the Bill was rushed through its final stages. It was not to be enforced until July, however, to allow for representations against it. This gave rise to a number of protest activities led by the NWCSA. On May 15th, for example, at Diamond Lodge, 28

40

Prince Alfred Street, San Fernando, a meeting was held, chaired by Elma Francois and with Clement Payne and Bertie Percival as main speakers.

In June 1938 a petition of the NWCSA was forwarded through Acting Governor J. Higgins to Malcolm MacDonald, Secretary of State for the Colonies. It strongly protested against the new ordinance as a serious inconvenience and hardship on the majority of the population. Approximately 4,620 signatures were attached, collected by NWCSA members walking from door to door. Of the signatures collected, over 1,000 were taken from domestic servants and 'housewives'.

Copies of resolutions passed at meetings were also forwarded along with copies of this petition. Two such are as follows:

(1)

His Excellency, Right Honourable
Malcolm MacDonald, M.P.,[27]
10 Downing Street,
London,
England.

The Negro Welfare Cultural
and Social Association,
66 George Street,
Port of Spain,
Trinidad, B.W.I.

July 12, 1938.

May it please Your Excellency this resolution was passed by the Workers and Citizens of Port of Spain assembled at 66 George Street on the night of July 7th, 1938 in public mass meeting convened by the above-mentioned Association.

Resolution: We view with grave concern the introduction of this new legislation known as the Shop Hours Ordinance, which aim is to create Big Business monopoly in favour of a few. This Bill has been hurried through, not giving time for protest and comment by the working classes of this island. There has been no demand from the workers for such a Bill. It is in the light of that reason we call upon you to withhold such Bill under the Statute of Westminster which guarantees the right to weak people.

(Sgd.)

Clement O. Payne
  Hon. Chairman
Adelaide Harrison
  Secretary
Elma Francois
  Org. Secretary
B. Percival
  Organiser

41

(2)   July 12th, 1938

His Excellency the Governor,[28]
Sir Hubert Wintrop Young, K.C.M.G.

Sir,
    At a meeting held at Diamond Lodge, San Fernando, Sunday 15th
May, the following resolution was passed by over 500 workers.
    We the workers and citizens of the town of San Fernando and
surrounding districts view with grave displeasure the Government's
attitude in passing the New Shop Hours Bill recently in the Legislative
Council and pledge our protest indignantly against any change whatever
in the present Ordinance as it now stands.
    We further emphasize in our protest in this public mass meeting that
if Government should proclaim the New Shop Hours Bill as Law, that
it will place us in grave inconveniences to make the necessary shopping
in harmony with the irregular hours and time in which we poor working
class get our pay, we therefore ask that a copy of this resolution be
forwarded to the Secretary of State for the Colonies asking him not to
approve of his Majesty's signature to the Bill.

                    (Sgd.)   Clement O. Payne
                                        Hon. Chairman
                                        Adelaide Harrison
                                        Secretary
                                        Elma Francois
                                        Org. Secretary
                                        B. Percival
                                        Organiser

Further protests were received from the Naparima Star Lodge
No. 2787, Loyal Order of Ancient Shepherds, the Ashton
Unity Friendly Society, Eastern Unity Friendly Society, San
Fernando, and the Workers Defence Committee of which the
NWCSA was a member.[29] Although support for these protests
came from rank and file workers, it was surprisingly not
forthcoming from the newly emerging trade unions. Already
these unions were possibly concentrating on their own con-
stituencies — the wage workers. We get some hint of this in
the Diary of John Jagger, member of the Oil Arbitration
Tribunal which visited Trinidad and Tobago in late 1938
and early 1939. His entry for Monday, December 19th 1938,
reads as follows:

We had an interesting interview with the E.C. of the Shop Assistants

42

Union again tonight, and found to our horror that they were proposing to start agitation against a new Shop Hours Regulation Bill on the grounds that it would penalise the small shopkeeper, but after wrestling with them in spirit we convinced them of the error of their ways.[30]

Thus the struggle against the Shop Hours Ordinance was denied the support of the Union of Shop Assistants and Clerks but it continued into early 1939. Rennie suggests that the passing of this Ordinance signalled the demise of small black business through bankruptcy and financial distress, and their replacement by Syrian and Jewish merchants, the latter fleeing Nazi persecution in Europe. In his own words;

> The Shop Closing Ordinance was only one of the many 'such unnatural means' throughout our history, depicting the efforts of the capitalists to maintain permanently the division of labour.[31]

Other Activities

Although the Shop Hours Bill agitation and the sedition trials took up a great amount of their energy in 1937-1938, NWCSA members still found time for other struggles.

In the aftermath of the 1937 disturbances, for example, together with members of Butler's BEW&CHRP, the Workers Defence Committee (WDC) was formed. The main aims of this committee were:

1. To collect money for legal defence for members facing numerous 'trumped up' charges, and to support the children of members in jail or killed during the disturbances.
2. To spread counter information and so frustrate police efforts to find Butler.
3. To organise public meetings to provide information throughout the country.[32]

In spite of their differences with Butler, as has been seen earlier, a great deal of emphasis was placed on support for Butler. In late September 1937 for example, after Butler had given himself up, the NWCSA called on oil workers to strike to press for the withdrawal of all charges against him. This call was rejected by the Oilfield Workers Trade Union executive. At a public meeting held at Reclaimed Lands, South Quay, on Tuesday, 28th September 1937, a resolution demanding Butler's release was passed.

43

In November 1938, in the 'run-up' to World War II, an attempt was made to control trade union power through the introduction of a new Masters and Servants Ordinance. One handbill, announcing a meeting on this issue, called on 'Workers of every Class' including intellectuals, trade unionists and domestic servants to protest. In spite of the action of workers and the NWCSA, however, the Bill was approved on December 8th 1938.

During 1938-39, solidarity with international struggles continued to be an important component of the NWCSA's activity. In this period, support for anti-fascist movements was important and was often linked to local struggles.

In September-October 1938 for example, the NWCSA gave solidarity and support to those of the local Chinese community who were mobilising local support against Japanese military actions in China. Support was also expressed for the Spanish workers movement struggling against the fascist forces of General Franco in alliance with Hitler. On the 29th September 1938 a mass meeting in solidarity with the Chinese people was held at No. 66 George Street, Port of Spain. This was followed by a United Peace Demonstration on Sunday, 9th October 1938 at 3.00 p.m. Demonstrations in support of the Spanish 'Workers Government' also took place.

These actions of international solidarity illustrate clearly the fact, referred to in the introduction to this study, that the affirmation of racial pride, in a society where to be black was considered to be a social disability, did not preclude joint action with anti-colonial, anti-imperialist people of other races and ethnic groups. A NWCSA pamphlet advertising a mass meeting on solidarity with the Chinese stated:

In this country we used to think of White Government as Bad Government which do harm to those who are not white. But in China today we see how a Government of yellow persons the Japanese is making an attempt to put chains on a yellow nation (the Chinese).

In Spain on the other hand we see how two White Governments (Germany and Italy) are making an attempt to put chains on a White Nation (Spain); and making use of Black military men (Moors) for this purpose. This proves to you that behaviour is not judged by the colour of skin; men and Governments have to be judged by what they do and not by their nation or language.

44

Come to No 66 George St.

TO-NIGHT,

Thursday, 1st December, 1938,

at 8 p.m. Sharp

Subject :

Masters & Servants Ordinance

It is worthy to note, THAT THIS BILL WHICH·HAD IT SECOND READING IN THE LEGISLATIVE COUNCIL ON FRIDAY LAST IS 93 Years Old. It w PASSED in THE Year 1846 THIS IS AN OLD TIE SLAVE LAW It is been revoked. But termed Reviewed TH BILL directly aims AT TRADE UNION MOVEMENT THE RIGHT TO STRIKE It was PASSED just after the abolition of SLAVERY

It comes at the Same Time when Hitler THE NAZI DICTATOR is Bellowing for the former German Colonies in Africa which would mean extermination of the negroes there the present campaign that has been waged against the Jews in Germany are glaring examples of the fate that await the negroes there. In the light of these experiences. We must protest.

WORKERS OF EVERY CLASS
INTELLECTUALS   TRADE   UNIONIST   DOMESTIC
SERVANT—COME!
AN OPEN LETTER WILL ALSO BE READ FROM
PROMINENT NEGROES FROM AFRICA.

ISSUED BY THE NEGRO WELFARE CULTURAL
ASSOCIATION,

45

The following year the NWCSA was able to show more concrete support. On August 22nd 1939, eleven Spanish refugees fleeing from France passed through Port of Spain in the sloop Alexandrina, which was a gift from the French workers. The sloop was met at the St. Vincent Street jetty by workers, sympathisers and NWCSA members and a statement against fascism was made. According to *The People*:

> Comrade Francois presented a basket of Trinidad fruits along with Trinidad Bay Rum, Limacol and baby foods. Comrades Goodridge and King also presented two baskets of Red Flowers to the female refugees ...[33]

In return, according to Rennie, the Spanish refugees presented to the NWCSA a picture of Black American anti-imperialist Paul Robeson singing to Spanish workers in the trenches.[34]

In 1939 also, the NWCSA re-activated the celebration of Emancipation Day on the 105th anniversary of abolition of slavery. That year celebrations took place at the St. Joseph's Road Children's Playground and included a treat for the 'poorer classes'. During the programme, Clement Payne spoke on the history of slavery, the slave trade and emancipation, while Councillor Alfred Richards 'appealed to mothers to educate their children while they were young on the political affairs of their country'.

For her part, Elma Francois identified June 19th 1937 as the date of the 'New Emancipation' which had spread throughout the West Indies. This date marked an era of new economic and industrial emancipation. This term 'New Emancipation' really encapsulated the new feelings of strength and confidence felt by the working classes after June 1937. For this reason the newsletter of the NWCSA launched at this time was entitled *The New Emancipator*.

In many ways this period marked the peak of the organisation's activity and Elma Francois' career. However, this was not the end and in spite of grave losses and much persecution they persevered.

The NWCSA and the Emergence of the Trade Union Movement
The significance of the NWCSA in the development of the early trade unions, in North Trinidad in particular, has until

recently[35] not been adequately recognised. Work with the trade unions, however, never formed the main focus of the organisation as a whole but certain members such as Dudley Mahon, Gaskynd Granger and Christopher Harper concentrated on work in trade unions.

The NWCSA can be associated with the emergence of almost every northern trade union during the period 1937-1940. As workers themselves, participation in the labour movement was often part of their struggles for improved conditions of life and work. Between 1935 and 1936, for example, when a number of workers on the shipping lines, including Christopher Harper, lost their jobs, it was to Jim Barrette, a port worker, and the NWCSA that they came for assistance in an effort to get relief through Capt. A.A. Cipriani. According to Christina King, it was as a means of occupying the time of the now 'idle' shipwrights that the 'Seamen's Social Club' was initially formed.

The NWCSA-organised May Day celebrations in 1937, therefore, involved a United Front May Day Committee including the Amalgamated Building and Woodworkers Union — No. 1 of San Juan and No. 2 of Port of Spain — and the Seamen's Social Club. In November that year, the Seamen and Waterfront Workers Trade Union (SWWTU) was registered with Jim Barrette as President and with headquarters at the corner of Duncan Street and Independence Square. It was known as the 'tamarind square union'.[36]

In July 1937, the Federated Workers Trade Union (FWTU) was formed by Alfred Richards and E. Mortimer Mitchell, the former a close colleague of the NWCSA. Later on the Union of Shop Assistants and Clerks (USAC), led by Quintin O'Connor and Albert Gomes, was incorporated into the Federated Workers Trade Union (FWTU) under their leadership. NWCSA member Dudley Mahon and later Negro Welfare youth movement member Joseph Grannum were both FWTU members. Because of the participation of Richards and later Gomes and O'Connor, as leading elected councillors, in the Port of Spain Municipal Council, municipal workers always made up a large proportion of the membership in the FWTU. In August 1937 another union, the Public Works and Public Service Workers Union (PW&PSWTU),

was formed with NWCSA member Gaskynd Granger as organiser and acting treasurer.

By May Day 1938, therefore, the May Day United Front Committee included the PW&PSWTU, FWTU, SWWTU and the NWCSA. Slogans at that May Day demonstration included: 'Long Live Butler!', 'Long Live the International!', 'Long Live Jim Barrette!' (then in prison on sedition charges), 'No Trinidad Oil for Franco!' and 'This is not Rhodesia!' It was on this occasion that, as the demonstration passed the jail, Barrette joined in the singing of the Internationale so loudly that a prison warden had to ask him to lower his voice.

On June 18th 1938, the NWCSA commemorated the events of June 19th 1937 by celebrating 'Butler's Day' at the SWWTU Hall, 54 George Street, Port of Spain. Representatives of the already mentioned unions were present and speakers included Clement Payne, Caesar Ashby, Bertie Percival and E. Mortimer Mitchell. The main address was given by Elma Francois. According to *The People*:

> Comrade Francois of the Negro Welfare Cultural and Social Association then delivered a most interesting address, giving a thrilling experience of her activities in South Trinidad during the strike and the disturbances that followed.[37]

Representatives of these unions as well as other individuals formed the nucleus of the Workers United Front Committee (WUFC), which, in the period 1938-39, mobilised against the Shop Hours Bill and submitted a memorandum on reform of the Constitution of Trinidad and Tobago.

The pre-war years of 1937-39 marked the culmination of the pre-war depression period. The issue of unemployment therefore continued to exist and in 1939 once more emerged as an issue for the working class. Once again the NWCSA returned to this familiar subject and joined with other unions in the Committee of Industrial Organisation (CIO) in a demonstration against unemployment. At the rally speakers included Elma Francois and OWTU/ATTGWTU* mobiliser Daisy Crick. Other activities on unemployment continued

---

*All Trinidad Transport and General Workers Trade Union — sister union of the Oilfields Workers Trade Union (OWTU).

into 1940 including the opening of a register of unemployed. The General Secretary Adelaide Harrison had the responsibility for the register.

So closely was the NWCSA associated with the trade unions that they were also on the receiving end of the efforts of the British Trade Union Congress and Fabian Colonial Bureau to institute 'responsible' trade unionism. In February 1939, the following letter was sent to Elma Francois and to other leading trade unionists:

11th February, 1939.[38]

Dear Miss Francois,
One of the problems confronting you in the building of a trade union organisation in your colony is inadequate information as to how the trade union movement in Great Britain works. Some years ago I attempted to give a brief account of the British Trade Union Movement. I enclose a copy. If you will pass it on to a few of your active officials and if they find it of some assistance to them, I will send out a few more copies.

Yours sincerely

A. Creech-Jones

By May Day 1939, the NWCSA demonstration included representatives of the All-Trinidad Sugar Estates and Factory Workers Trade Union and of the San Juan Sanatan Association. On this occasion the theme of racial unity was taken up by the speakers who included Elma Francois.

Days after this T.U.B. Butler was freed from prison to a tumultuous welcome throughout the country. Welcome celebrations culminated in a mammoth thanksgiving at the Queen's Park Savannah. The platform included Daisy Crick and Elma Francois. At this meeting the old tensions between Butler and the NWCSA surfaced over their disagreement as to what position the Trinidad and Tobago workers should take in relation to the upcoming war.

By June 1940, World War II having been declared, T.U.B. Butler was once more detained in prison, this time on Nelson Island where he remained for the entire duration of the war. In spite of their differences, the NWCSA participated in Butler Day celebrations on June 23rd at La Brea that year. In her speech on this occasion Elma Francois revealed that the NWCSA remained in close contact with Butler.

Relations with the trade unions continued throughout the NWCSA's existence in varying degrees. The tendency of the union leaders to deny their socialist links was however viewed with dismay. In La Brea in June 1940, Francois publicly attacked Quintin O'Connor, and trade union leaders in general, for severing their links with the workers' movement, from whence they emerged, after they had become established.

CHAPTER VI

The Death of Elma Francois and the NWCSA in its Twilight Years

The immediate pre-war period saw an intensification of the economic conditions which contributed to the labour disturbances of 1937. In addition, the increased repression of radical labour and political organisations combined to make this a difficult period for the working class.

In spite of this, the confidence generated in 1937 served to facilitate the blossoming of the labour and radical political movement. At the same time more of the sons of the middle classes began to participate in the popular movements, and eventually took over control of these organisations. Daughters, however, were usually confined to social work activities such as those of the Coterie of Social Workers.

In 1939, within the spirit of impending 'self-government', the NWCSA submitted a memorandum on constitutional reform to Malcolm MacDonald, Secretary of State for the Colonies. Signatories to the memorandum included women members Elma Francois, Organising Secretary, and Adelaide Harrison, Financial Secretary. This memorandum, among other things, supported the widening of the franchise and the removal of non-elected representatives in the Legislature The NWCSA's memorandum received no response from the colonial powers.

On the labour scene, increased unemployment coincided with the attempts of the colonial officials and local capitalists to control the growing power of the workers' movement.

In January 1939, the earlier practice of unemployed Hunger Marches emerged once again. Workers being laid off in the 'Oilfields' were told to 'go to the Union for jobs'. At one such march in March 1939 organised by the Committee for Industrial Organisation (CIO), the forerunner of the Trinidad and Tobago Trade Union Congress (T&TTUC), platform speakers included Elma Francois and Daisy Crick. The problems of unemployment continued into 1940 and numerous demonstrations and actions occurred, including requests for the dole. In August 1940, the NWCSA organised a register of unemployed at the corner of Laventille Road and Piccadilly Street, coordinated by Adelaide Harrison, their General Secretary.

The issue of World War II was to be a major factor in dividing and weakening the workers' movement. The NWCSA held the view, which was strongly put forward by its ideologue Elma Francois, that Caribbean colonial subjects should not participate in the imperialist war. This unpopular position served to further isolate the NWCSA.

In March 1939, for example, at the thanksgiving for his release at the Queen's Park Savannah, T.U.B. Butler pledged his loyalty to the British Empire and exhorted workers to fight against Nazism. NWCSA members on the platform — Elma Francois, Clement Payne and Jim Barrette — publicly disagreed with this position. As far as they were concerned, the Western allies had initially seen Hitler's rise as a counter to Stalin in the Soviet Union. It was only when Hitler turned his military might against them that they sought to defend themselves and draw in colonials, whom they discriminated against racially, to die with them in their war.

There is evidence that popular opinion at the beginning of the war was anti-British. In his autobiography, *Through A Maze of Colour*,[39] Albert Gomes noted that cinema crowds clapped during shows when the British were defeated by the fascists. By 1940, however, colonial propaganda had intensified to the degree where loyalty to the Crown became the dominant outlook on the war. In spite of *his* loyalty, however, Butler was re-arrested in early 1940 under wartime defence regulations. Leading the campaign for his release were NWCSA members including Elma Francois.

In 1940 repression by the colonial regime intensified. The editor of *Picong*, Jean de Boissiere, was charged with libel; the *Trinidad Guardian* called for an enquiry into alleged subversive activity; the office of *The People* newspaper was searched; the home of Albert Gomes, then a member of the Port of Spain City Council and an active trade unionist, was searched. In July, Cipriani accused the Public Library of importing anti-British and leftist books and two Irish teachers, Frank Cahill and Kay Donnellan, active in the trade union movement, were fired from their jobs at St. Joseph's Convent. In addition, as would be expected, the NWCSA was accused of helping Hitler win the war.

In the rest of 1940 NWCSA activities continued to focus on unemployment and they joined with other trade unions in fighting City Council elections. These same trade unions, led by middle-class 'progressives', had, in 1939, pledged their loyalty to the British throne and agreed to maintain industrial peace for the duration of the war. More and more, as the NWCSA sought to join the mainstream of political activity in the country it found increasingly that this had to be done through younger middle-class political activists who were less grounded in the workers' movement.

It was at this time also that Elma Francois' participation in public activity appears to have diminished. She developed goitre and, with it, a fear of going to the doctor.

It was at this time also that Elma Francois received a shock which, some feel, contributed to her early death. Her only son Conrad, who had joined her in Trinidad and Tobago a few years earlier, decided to join the British army and leave for the front. In the words of her comrade and companion Jim Barrette:

> She was very shocked when her son told her. We were taking tea in the gallery. He told her he had a citation and he was going to the barracks, she must come to the parade ... She did not drink any more tea. She said — I have tried so hard with this boy but I told her she had no more jurisdiction over him. I tried to explain to him how she felt and he walked away...
>
> She insisted on going to the parade and I went with her. She was crying and I had to help her as she couldn't take it any more ... They marched all over the city, to the Savannah for the people to become war conscious — people were throwing kisses ...[40]

The above illustrates clearly the contradictions often faced by parents in bringing up children in a society whose beliefs run counter to their own principles and aspirations; the pain which she felt illustrates the degree to which her daily political struggle was a deeply lived aspect of her very being.

For his part, Conrad states he always had a love for war.

53

During his mother's visit to St. Vincent in 1926-27 she had once given him a penny. He used this to purchase a packet of pins which, to his mother's horror, he set out like an army. He recalls the sweets during the early war years with slogans such as 'I like war' because he liked war and even wore war slogans on his shirt. He eventually applied to join the navy, but in May 1943 was drafted into the army at a salary of $5.04 per week, less than he had been previously earning at the docks.

Just under one year later he received his citation to leave for the front and he was confined to barracks. On April 16th 1944, Francois attended the farewell dance at the Princes Building to say goodbye to her only son. Although not a dancer, she danced with him at his request. It was the last time he saw her alive.[41]

Her death came suddenly the following day. She had finally agreed to visit nurse Goodridge in Morvant, but while sleeping she had an attack. Again in Jim's words:

> I was at Alfred Richard's and the day was so hot I decided to take an ice cream for her at home, but when I arrived she jumped at me...[42]

The news reached Conrad, then confined to barracks, but he managed to get permission to leave. That night he went to the house with his mother's friends and attended the funeral on the following day. He then set sail for the war in Europe and North Africa.

Her comrades remained convinced that her death was triggered off by the grief of her only son's decision, which went against everything she stood for. This is possible as stress can negatively affect diseases of the thyroid.

As with other NWCSA members, Francois received a 'socialist' funeral. The body, dressed in a red shroud, was displayed at the home of a neighbour on St. Paul Street, before being taken through the streets of Port of Spain to the Woodbrook cemetery. NWCSA members all wore their full uniform of red blouses or shirts, flannel trousers or skirts and red felt or panama hats. Among those watching the procession walk along Piccadilly Street was Captain A.A. Cipriani. The parting address at the graveside was given by Bertie Percival.

54

After Francois

During World War II NWCSA activities like all others were curtailed, especially as member Dudley Mahon was detained with Cahill and Donnellan under wartime regulations. In 1944 the Negro Welfare Cultural and Industrial Youth Movement was formed, at various times under the patronage of Alfred Richards, Tito Achong, T.U.B. Butler, Bhadase Maraj and Raymond Quevedo. Youth members included Carl Pratt, Joseph Grannum, Merle Dowers and the Secretary was Amy Dowers.

Emancipation Day celebrations on 1st August every year at Columbus Square in Port of Spain was one of the main activities and this continued under the auspices of the Youth Movement. And in spite of the name, it was noted that membership included 'Negroes, Indians and Chinese'. Membership however decreased rapidly during the anti-communist scare of the early 1950s.

In the post-war period, NWCSA members were never able to regain the momentum which they had previously. The development of trade unionism, largely influenced by the British Trade Union Congress and very much under the control of the middle class, led to a decline in their importance. In many ways NWCSA members themselves such as Christopher Harper recognised their inability to deal with the new situation although new strategies were explored.

In 1946, for example, the NWCSA participated in the discussions leading to the formation of the United Front for the first general election held under universal adult suffrage. And in 1945, Christopher Lynch had represented the organisation at the important 5th Pan-African Congress organised by George Padmore, Amy Ashwood Garvey and C.L.R. James in London.

It was around this time that the main remaining members of the NWCSA, Jim Barrette, Christina King and Lucius Mondezie, joined with the Marxist study class movement to form the Workers Freedom Movement.

In the 1940s Marxist study groups were formed in Port of Spain, in Point Fortin and in San Fernando. The group in Port of Spain included some young civil servants and workers. This group split in the late 1940s over the issue of whether to participate or not in public political activity. After this split, the study group remained with three workers — Osmund Fletcher, Llewellyn Cross and Felix — and two others, and continued to meet. It was this study group that John La Rose joined after it had split.

Several meetings and some time later the four members of that group — Cross, Felix, Fletcher and La Rose — on the initiative of Llewellyn Cross and with the support of Felix, decided to approach Jim Barrette and Christina King of the NWCSA to form a new organisation. After some discussion it was agreed not to retain the name of Negro Welfare Cultural and Social Association, as that name would not now historically represent our objectives, but to call our organisation the Workers Freedom Movement. The WFM also united within a single organisation with the Point Fortin Marxist study group.

The NWCSA continued in diminished form and was mainly concerned with the annual celebration of the 1st August as Emancipation Day, the day the African slaves had brought about their freedom from slavery. The NWCSA was concerned that 1st August was being celebrated as Discovery Day, the day that Columbus so-called 'discovered' Trinidad, instead of its being celebrated each year as Emancipation Day.* The NWCSA was determined to keep fresh the memory of the African slaves struggle for their freedom.

The WFM later united in 1952 with the leadership and some of the militant membership of three of the leading trade unions in Trinidad and Tobago — the Oilfields Workers Trade Union led by John Rojas, the Federated Workers Trade Union led by Quintin O'Connor and the All Trinidad Sugar Estates and Factory Workers Trade Union led by Oli Mohammed — to form the West Indian Independence Party.

The WIIP at its inception included in its executive leadership John Rojas as Vice Chairman and Quintin O'Connor as Treasurer, as well as Oli Mohammed, John Poon and Jim Barrette. The Chairman was Lennox Pierre and John La Rose was General Secretary. Among the leading members of the WIIP in South Trinidad were George Weekes, George Bowrin, James Cummings and Christina Lewis, who later formed the Caribbean Women's National Assembly.[43]

The WIIP felt the weight of Cold War repression in the Caribbean. This led to the overthrow of the elected Peoples Progressive Party government led by Cheddi Jagan, in Guyana in 1953 by British troops only 133 days after it had taken office. Then came the publication of the Dalley Report in Trinidad in 1954, whose aim was the separation of the labour movement from the radical political organisations. This aim

---

* Since 1984 August 1st has been celebrated in Trinidad and Tobago as Emancipation Day and is a public holiday.

56

was largely, though not completely, achieved, and most of the trade union leadership and militants were compelled to split off from the WIIP in late 1953.

The WIIP contested the 1956 election with just one candidate.

This participation was largely symbolic and was intended to highlight the constitutional issue of the Right to Recall, that is the electors right to recall and remove an elected representative and subject him or her to a new election if he failed to satisfy his electors by his representation.

The candidate was John La Rose because of his support among tenant farmers and some industrial workers in the East St George constituency. The WIIP lost its deposit. Another reason for the WIIP's very limited participation in the elections was to expose the pro-imperialist tendencies in the PNM and to indicate a workers and peoples platform for change. [44]

This election, won by the Peoples National Movement, represented the culmination of the emergence of middle-strata nationalism which characterised the period of the late 1940s and 1950s. These new, less radical, nationalists sought to keep their distance from the radical workers movement which had championed the cause of the working class and independence for many years. The cause of labour and socialism to which Elma Francois and her comrades had dedicated their lives had now been overtaken by forces with clearly different political and social objectives, and the historic contribution of Elma Francois and her comrades to change in Trinidad and Tobago remained virtually forgotten until now.

On September 25 1987, the day in which Trinidad and Tobago celebrates Republic Day, Elma Francois was declared a National Heroine of Trinidad and Tobago.

Appendix

THE AIMS OF THE
NEGRO WELFARE CULTURAL AND SOCIAL ASSOCIATION *

a) To develop the economic standard and promote a progressive political outlook for the working class.

b) To develop solidarity with the oppressed Negro of the West Indies and the entire world.

c) To struggle for freedom of speech, assembly and press.

d) For the full rights of Trade Unions and Peasant organisations, a minimum of labour and social legislations, universal adult suffrage and democratic representative institutions.

e) To make known the conditions of the oppressed Negro people and their sufferings against oppression.

f) To win the masses of the oppressed people the world over in struggle for the better welfare of the Negro people.

g) To bring young people of all nations unto bonds of close friendship, to develop mutual understanding between youth of different races, religions and opinions.

h) To point out the economic and cultural status of youth and its relation to peace.

i) Extension of educational and economic opportunities for young people, reforms necessary concerning education, industry, crime, unemployment, health and leisure.

j) To plan methods of collaboration which will enable young people to fulfil their responsibility in contributing to world peace.

k) To promote, support or oppose any candidate on election to Legislative, Municipal, Borough Council or Boards, any Bill or Law which in the opinion of the Executive or Management Committee of this Association ought to be promoted, supported or opposed in the interest of the Association and the masses.

*Taken from *The Rules of the Negro Cultural and Social Association* and quoted in T. Henderson, The Role of Women in Politics in Trinidad and Tobago, Caribbean Studies Project 1973, U.W.I., St. Augustine, p. 22.

Notes

1. John LaGuerre, *The Politics of Communalism: The Agony of the Left in Trinidad and Tobago 1930-1955*, Pan Caribbean Publications (Revised Edition), 1982, pp. 31-32.
2. Interview with Jim Barrette and Christina King No 1, 1980; Wendy Charles, *Early Labour Organisation in Trinidad and the Butler Riots*, Working Papers on Caribbean Society, Sociology Dept., U.W.I., St. Augustine, 1978.
3. There was a deportation hearing in Trinidad which seems to have been concerned with Rupert Gittens' re-entry into Trinidad.
4. Interview with Dudley Mahon, 10th August 1982.
5. Bukka Rennie, *The History of the Working Class in the 20th Century (1919-1956) — the Trinidad and Tobago Experience*, Tunapuna, New Beginning Movement, 1973, p. 67.
6. Robert G. Weisbord, 'British West Indian Reaction to the Italian-Ethiopian War: An Episode in Pan Africanism' in *Caribbean Studies*, Vol. 10, No. 1.
7. Rennie, *op. cit.* (5), p. 53.
8. As sung to me on numerous occasions by Jim Barrette.
9. Rennie, *op. cit.* (5), p. 72.
10. Interview, Jim Barrette and Christina King No. 1, 1980.
11. Interview, Jim Barrette and Christina King, No. 2, 18th December 1981.
12, Ibid.
13. *The People*, 2nd January 1937, p. 4.
14. *The People*, 13th June 1936, p. 2.
15. Rennie, *op. cit.* (5), p. 91.
16. *The People*, 19th June 1937, p. 2.
17. Interview, Conrad James, 28th January 1987.
18. *Trinidad Guardian*, 23rd June 1937, p. 4.
19. *Trinidad Guardian*, 13th July 1937, p. 1.
20. *The People*, 2nd October 1937, p. 7.
21. *Trinidad Guardian*, 16th February 1938 and 17th February 1938, p. 2.
22. *Trinidad Guardian*, 15th February 1938, p. 2, 'Defence Opens in City Women Sedition Trial'.
23. *Trinidad Guardian*, 16th February 1938, p. 2, 'Judge to Sum Up This Morning in Women Sedition Trial'.
24. Arthur Calder Marshall, *Glory Dead*, Michael Joseph Ltd., London, 1939, p. 206.
25. Idem as above.

26. *The People*, 14th May 1938, pp. 4 & 8.
27. Enclosures in Letter from J. Higgins, Acting Governor, to Malcolm MacDonald, MP, on representations received re: The Shop Hours of Opening and Employment Ordinance, CO 295/607, File No. 70380.
28. Ibid as above.
29. Ibid as above.
30. John Jagger, Trinidad and the Tribunal: A Descriptive Diary, November 1938 — February 1939, p. 29.
31. Rennie, *op. cit.* (5), p. 21.
32. Ibid., pp. 96-100.
33. *The People*, 9th August 1939, p. 9.
34. Rennie, *op. cit.* (5), p. 125.
35. See Ron Ramdin, *From Chattel Slave to Wage Earner*, Martin, Brian and O'Keefe, London, 1982, pp. 141-142.
36. Interview with Jim Barrette and Christina King, 16th October 1985.
37. *The People*, 2nd July 1938, p. 5.
38. Arthur Creech-Jones Papers, Trinidad 1937-1939, Box 25 File 4, File 1-4, Rhodes House Library, Colonial Manuscripts Collection, Oxford.
39. Albert Gomes, *Through a Maze of Colour*, Key Caribbean Publications, 1974, p. 57.
40. Interview with Jim Barrette and Christina King, 25th January 1987.
41. Interview with Conrad James, 28th January 1987.
42. Interview with Jim Barrette and Christina King, 25th January 1987.
43. Information supplied by John La Rose.
44. Ibid, John La Rose.